First World War
and Army of Occupation
War Diary
France, Belgium and Germany

42 DIVISION
127 Infantry Brigade,
Brigade Trench Mortar Battery
1 April 1917 - 31 December 1918

WO95/2661/4

The Naval & Military Press Ltd
www.nmarchive.com
Published in association with The National Archives

Published by

The Naval & Military Press Ltd

Unit 10 Ridgewood Industrial Park,

Uckfield, East Sussex,

TN22 5QE England

Tel: +44 (0) 1825 749494

www.naval-military-press.com

www.nmarchive.com

This diary has been reprinted in facsimile from the original. Any imperfections are inevitably reproduced and the quality may fall short of modern type and cartographic standards.

© **Crown Copyright**
Images reproduced by permission of The National Archives, London, England, 2015.

Contents

Document type	Place/Title	Date From	Date To
Heading	WO95/2661/4 127 Inf Bgde Bgde T.M. Battery Apr'17-Dec'18		
Heading	42nd Division 127th Infy Bde Lt. Trench Mortar Bty Apr 1917-Dec 1918		
Heading	War Diary Of 127th Brigade Light Trench Mortar Battery. From. 1st April 1917 To 30th April 1917 (Volume 1)		
War Diary	Montigny	01/04/1917	14/04/1917
War Diary	Vaux-En-Amienois	14/04/1917	23/04/1917
War Diary	Peronne	24/04/1917	30/04/1917
Heading	War Diary Of 127 Light Trench Mortar Battery From 1st May To 30th May 1917 Volume 1		
War Diary	Villers Faucon	01/05/1917	09/05/1917
War Diary	Longavesnes	10/05/1917	17/05/1917
War Diary	Neuville	18/05/1917	20/05/1917
War Diary	Ruyaulcourt	21/05/1917	31/05/1917
Heading	127th Light Trench Mortar Battery June To December 1917		
Heading	175th Brigade Orders		
Heading	War Diary Of 127th Light Trench Mortar Battery From June 1st To 30th 1917 Vol 1		
War Diary	Ruyaulcourt	01/06/1917	22/06/1917
War Diary	Havrincourt Wood	23/06/1917	30/06/1917
Heading	War Diary Of The 127th Light Trench Mortar Battery From July 1st To July 31st 1917 Volume 1		
War Diary	Havrincourt Wood	01/07/1917	08/07/1917
War Diary	Barastre	09/07/1917	09/07/1917
War Diary	Achiet	10/07/1917	31/07/1917
Heading	War Diary Of The 127th Light Trench Mortar Battery For August 1917 Volume 1		
War Diary	Achiet	01/08/1917	20/08/1917
War Diary	Aveluy	21/08/1917	21/08/1917
War Diary	Poperinghe	22/08/1917	31/08/1917
Heading	War Diary Of The 127th Light Trench Mortar Battery From Sept 1st 1917 To Sept 30th 1917 Volume 1		
War Diary	Poperinghe	01/09/1917	06/09/1917
War Diary	Ypres D.8	07/09/1917	14/09/1917
War Diary	Poperinghe (C.8.)	15/09/1917	19/09/1917
War Diary	Winnezeele (B.8.)	20/09/1917	21/09/1917
War Diary	Coxyde (B.6.)	22/09/1917	30/09/1917
Heading	War Diary Of The 127th Light Trench Mortar Battery From October 1st 1917 To October 31st 1917 Volume 1		
War Diary	Coxyde	01/10/1917	21/10/1917
War Diary	Nieuport	22/10/1917	31/10/1917
War Diary	Nieuport	23/10/1917	31/10/1917
Heading	War Diary Of The 127th Light Trench Mortar Battery From November 1st 1917 To November 30th 1917 Volume. 2		
War Diary	Nieuport (C.6.)	01/11/1917	07/11/1917
War Diary	Canada Camp (B.6.)	08/11/1917	16/11/1917

War Diary	Leffrinckoucke (A.6.)	17/11/1917	17/11/1917
War Diary	Wormhoudt (A.8.)	18/11/1917	18/11/1917
War Diary	Rietveld	19/11/1917	19/11/1917
War Diary	Oxeleare (A.9)	20/11/1917	20/11/1917
War Diary	Berguette (A.10.)	21/11/1917	26/11/1917
War Diary	Vendin (B.11)	27/11/1917	27/11/1917
War Diary	Givenchy (C.11.)	28/11/1917	30/11/1917
Heading	War Diary Of The 127th Light Trench Mortar Battery From December 1st /1917 To December 31st /1917 Volume 1		
War Diary	Festubert (C 11)	01/12/1917	22/12/1917
War Diary	Bethune	22/12/1917	28/12/1917
War Diary	Obwnghem	28/12/1917	31/12/1917
Heading	War Diary Of 127th Light Trench Mortar Bty. For Jan.1918 Vol. II		
War Diary	Oblinghem	01/01/1918	03/01/1918
War Diary	Beuvry	03/01/1918	31/01/1918
Heading	War Diary Of The 127th Light Trench Mortar Battery From February 1st /1918 February 28th /1918 Volume. 2		
War Diary	Beuvry	01/02/1918	12/02/1918
War Diary	Burbure	12/02/1918	28/02/1918
Heading	42nd Division. 127th Infantry Brigade. 127th Light Trench Mortar Battery March 1918		
War Diary	Burbure 36 A S.W. 1/20000	01/03/1918	04/03/1918
War Diary	Busnes 36 A S. E 1/20,000	04/03/1918	23/03/1918
War Diary	Ayette 57D 1/40,000	24/03/1918	24/03/1918
War Diary	Gomiecourt	25/03/1918	25/03/1918
War Diary	Ablainzevelle	26/03/1918	26/03/1918
War Diary	Fonquevillers	26/03/1918	27/03/1918
War Diary	Essarts Le Bucquoy	28/03/1918	30/03/1918
Heading	127th Inf. Bde. 42nd Div. 127th Light Trench Mortar Battery. April 1918		
Heading	War Diary Of The 127th Light Trench Mortar Battery From April 1st /1918 To April 30th /1918 Volume 2		
War Diary	Essarts Le Bucquoy	01/04/1918	03/04/1918
War Diary	Ablainzeville (J.5.)	04/04/1918	08/04/1918
War Diary	Louvencourt (F.5.)	09/04/1918	15/04/1918
War Diary	Louvencourt	09/04/1918	16/04/1918
War Diary	Hebuterne	17/04/1918	24/04/1918
War Diary	Bayencourt	25/04/1918	28/04/1918
War Diary	Gommecourt	29/04/1918	30/04/1918
Heading	War Diary Of The 127th Light Trench Mortar Battery From 1st May 1918 To 31st May 1918 Volume 2		
War Diary	Gommecourt H. 5	01/05/1918	05/05/1918
War Diary	Henu D 19	06/05/1918	31/05/1918
War Diary	Henu	01/06/1918	05/06/1918
War Diary	Hebuterne	06/06/1918	14/06/1918
War Diary	Bus Woods	15/06/1918	23/06/1918
War Diary	In The Line	24/06/1918	30/06/1918
Heading	War Diary Of The 127th Light Trench Mortar Battery From July 1st 1918 To July 31st 1918 Volume 2		
War Diary	In The Line (Battery H.Q J 24 D)	01/07/1918	10/07/1918
War Diary	Bus Woods (J 2 D C)	10/07/1918	18/07/1918
War Diary	In The Line (Battery H Q At J 17.C.)	18/07/1918	03/08/1918
War Diary	Bus Woods (J. 20.C)	04/08/1918	11/08/1918

War Diary	In The Line (Right Sector)		12/08/1918	24/08/1918
War Diary	Miraumont		25/08/1918	25/08/1918
War Diary	Pys		26/08/1918	27/08/1918
War Diary	In The Line (Battery H.Q. M.6. Central)		28/08/1918	31/08/1918
Heading	War Diary Of The 127th Light Trench Mortar Battery From September 1st/1918 To September 30th/1918 Volume 2			
War Diary	In The Line (Battery H.Q. M.6. Central)		01/09/1918	01/09/1918
War Diary	In The Line (H.Q.N.4.A.5.9.)		02/09/1918	04/09/1918
War Diary	In The Line (Support Bde)		05/09/1918	05/09/1918
War Diary	Little Wood (M.9.d.9.9.)		06/09/1918	07/09/1918
War Diary	Warlencourt M.10.B.4.7		08/09/1918	20/09/1918
War Diary	Bertincourt P.2.d.2.8		21/09/1918	25/09/1918
War Diary	K.31.B.6.5		26/09/1918	26/09/1918
War Diary	In The Line (Batty. H.Q. K.31.B.6.5)		27/09/1918	29/09/1918
War Diary	P.11.A.9.4		30/09/1918	30/09/1918
Heading	War Diary Of The 127th Light Trench Mortar Battery From October 1st/1918 To October 31st/1918 Volume 2			
War Diary	P 11 A.9.4		01/10/1918	08/10/1918
War Diary	Villers Plouich Map Rfce Sheet 57 B 1:40,000		09/10/1918	09/10/1918
War Diary	Esnes		10/10/1918	13/10/1918
War Diary	Beauvois (I 10.)		14/10/1918	18/10/1918
War Diary	Aulicourt Farm (I.1.A)		19/10/1918	19/10/1918
War Diary	Marou (S.E C Solesmes)		20/10/1918	21/10/1918
War Diary	Aulicourt Farm (I 1.A)		22/10/1918	22/10/1918
War Diary	Beauvois (I.10)		23/10/1918	31/10/1918
War Diary	Beauvois (5.E.)		01/11/1918	03/11/1918
War Diary	Viesley (5.F)		04/11/1918	04/11/1918
War Diary	Vertigneul Farm (4.G)		05/11/1918	05/11/1918
War Diary	Fme Du Lion (4.C)		06/11/1918	06/11/1918
War Diary	Maison Rouge (4.C)		07/11/1918	08/11/1918
War Diary	Vieux Mesnil (3 K)		09/11/1918	13/11/1918
War Diary	Hautmont (3.L)		14/11/1918	30/11/1918
Heading	War Diary Of The 127th Light Trench Mortar Battery From November 1st/1918 To November 30th/1918 Volume 2			
Heading	War Diary For 127th L T M Battery 1st-31st December 1918 Volume 12			
War Diary	Hautmont (Ref. Sheet Valcencienne 1.100,000 3 B)		01/12/1918	13/12/1918
War Diary	Hautmont		14/12/1918	14/12/1918
War Diary	Boussois (3A)		15/12/1918	15/12/1918
War Diary	Merbes. St Maire (2C)		16/12/1918	16/12/1918
War Diary	Leval Trahegnies (1C)		17/12/1918	17/12/1918
War Diary	Leval Trahegnies		18/12/1918	18/12/1918
War Diary	Marchiennes Au Pont		19/12/1918	19/12/1918
War Diary	Fleurus (1G)		20/12/1918	31/12/1918

WO 95/2661 (4)

127 INF BdDE

BdDE T. M. Battery

Apr '17 - Dec '18

42ND DIVISION
127TH INFY BDE

LT. TRENCH MORTAR BTY
APR 1917-DEC 1918

Original Vol 57

Confidential.

War Diary

of

127th Brigade Light Trench Mortar Battery.

From: 1st April 1917,
To 30th April 1917

(Volume 1.)

Apr '17
Dec '18

WAR DIARY INTELLIGENCE SUMMARY.

(Erase heading not required.)

Original PAGE 1.

Army Form C. 2118.

Place	Date	Hour	Summary of Events and Information	Remarks and references to Appendices
MONTIGNY	1/14th April 1917	—	Training at Third Corps School (Reference Sheet, AMIENS 17, 2nd ED., F.1.) France 1/100,000	S/1-1.
"	14/4/17	—	Battery moved to Fourth Army School of Mortars at VAUX-EN-AMIENOIS (Reference Sheet, AMIENS 17, 2nd ED., D.1.) Transport provided - two motor-busses, one motor-lorry. It was necessary for one lorry to make a double journey to carry hand carts.	S/1-1.
VAUX-EN-AMIENOIS	14/22nd 4/17	—	Battery training (Reference, Sheet, AMIENS 17, 2nd ED, D.1.)	S/1-1.
"	23/4/17	—	Battery moved to PERONNE (Rfce, Sheet No 4, N.W. EUROPE, D.6.) to join Brigade. Left VAUX-EN-AMIENOIS at 2 p.m., arrived PERONNE at 6.30 p.m. Transport provided - one motor bus and two motor lorries, personnel on bus and one lorry, stores on the other lorry. Loading party of one N.C.O. and three men left at school to bring along hand carts when another lorry should arrive for them.	S/1-1.
PERONNE	24/4/17	—	Battery doing fatigues under Town Major (Rfce, Sheet No 4, N.W. EUROPE, D.6.)	S/1-1.
"	25/4/17	—	— do — do — do —	S/1-1.
"	26/4/17	—	— do — do — do —	S/1-1.
"	27/4/17	—	— do — do — do —	S/1-1.

WAR DIARY or INTELLIGENCE SUMMARY

Army Form C. 2118.

PAGE 2.

Place	Date	Hour	Summary of Events and Information	Remarks and references to Appendices
PERONNE	27/4/17	—	Loading party with handcarts on one motor lorry arrived at 3 A.M.	S/H.
"	28/4/17	—	Fatigues as on previous days.	S/1-1.
"	29/4/17	—	— do — do —	S/1-1.
"	30/4/17	—	Battery moved to VILLERS (Rfce. Sheet No. 4. N.W. EUROPE, E.6.) and relieved the 126th French Mortar Battery. Left PERONNE at 9 A.M., arrived VILLERS at 1.30 p.m. Transport provided - one lorry for stores. Personnel marched with handcarts. Five handcarts were left in care of Town Major PERONNE, there being no transport for them and the personnel being insufficient to pull sixteen of them. 2ND LIEUT. LANDON with 13 other ranks proceeded to EPÉHY (Rfce, Sheet No. 4, N.W. EUROPE, E.5.) and relieved two detachments of 126th French Mortar Battery, taking over two of their guns. He took up a defensive position there. Battery handed over two guns to 126th Battery in exchange, to obviate necessity of carrying guns to positions (5 kilometres distant)	S/1-1.

S/ Hawkeslapte
O/C 127th T.M. Battery.

Confidential

War Diary

of

107 Light Trench Mortar Battery

from 1st May to 30th May 1917

Volume 1

WAR DIARY or INTELLIGENCE SUMMARY

Army Form C. 2118.

Place	Date	Hour	Summary of Events and Information	Remarks and references to Appendices
Villers FAUCON	1/5/17	-	Reference, Sheet No 4, N.W. EUROPE. E.6. 2nd Lt LANDON improved Position at EPÉHY. (Reference, Sheet No 4, N.W. EUROPE. E.5.) remainder of Battery improved billets and trained at VILLERS (Reference, as above)	D.H.
do	2/5/17	-	One N.C.O and fifteen men attached to the Battery over War establishment	D.H.
do	3/5/17	-	Battery training was carried on	D.H.
do	4/5/17	-	2nd Lt D.R NORMAN with 20 O.R. relieved 2nd Lt LANDON at EPÉHY (Rfce, as above)	D.H.
do	5/5/17	-	2nd Lt D.R. NORMAN with his party, worked on the picket line, 2,000 yards east of EPÉHY, excavating Gun implacements.	D.H.
do	6/5/17	-		
do	7/5/17	-		
do	8/5/17	-		
do	9/5/17	-	Battery was relieved by 125th Trench Mortar Battery and proceeded to Billets at LONGAVESNES (Rfce, Sheet No 4, N.W.EUROPE, E.6.) Left VILLERS at 1 p.m. arrived LONGAVESNES 2·30 p.m. Transport provided — One G.S. Wagon which made two journeys, personnel marched with eleven handcarts	D.H.
LONGAVESNES	10/5/17	-	(Rfce, Sheet No 4 N.W. EUROPE. E.6.) Improving Billets and cleaning up	D.H.
do	11/5/17	-	Battery carried out a demonstration, of a Stokes Mortar Barrage for the benefit of the Brigade, eight Guns were used, and 260 rounds of ammunition. Sight of demonstration, 1000 yds S.W. of LONGAVESNES	D.H.

WAR DIARY or INTELLIGENCE SUMMARY

Army Form C. 2118.

Place	Date	Hour	Summary of Events and Information	Remarks and references to Appendices
LONGAVESNES	12/5/17 to 16/5/17	-	The Battery trained (Gun Drill & Infantry Exercises), supplied fatigues to the Town Major, and the Box Respirators were tested at the Divisional Gas School, LONGAVESNES.	D.H.I.
do	17/5/17	-	Battery moved to NEUVILLE (Ref. Sheet No.4, N.W. EUROPE, D5) left LONGAVESNES at 5 a.m., arrived NEUVILLE at 12 noon. Transport provided - two and a half G.S. Wagons, personnel marched with eleven handcarts.	D.H.I.
NEUVILLE	18/5/17	-	(Ref. Sheet No.4, N.W. EUROPE, D5) Battery improved Billets and an inspection was carried out of all Arms & Kit.	D.H.I.
do	19/5/17	-	Battery stores were transported to RUYAULCOURT (Ref. Sheet No.4, N.W. EUROPE, D5) One G.S. Wagon was employed and made a double journey. Lt. D.H. SAYERS with a party of fifteen, left Billets at 8 p.m. to relieve three detachments of the 61st Trench Mortar Battery in the trenches north of HAVRINCOURT WOOD (Ref. D6). Three mortars of the 61st Trench Mortar Battery were taken over in the line and three of our own were handed over to them at RUYAULCOURT relief complete 10-30. The Mortars are in a position to defend our front line.	D.H.I.
do	20/5/17	-	Remaining personnel of Battery moved to RUYAULCOURT. (Ref. Chaghot, N.W. EUROPE D5.)	D.H.I.
RUYAULCOURT	21/5/17	-	Battery supplied fatigues under the R.E. and in the line.	D.H.I.
	22/5/17	-	2nd Lt. J.H. LANDON with a party of sixteen relieved Lt. D.H. SAYERS in the line taking over the Guns and all spare parts.	D.H.I.
	23/5/17 24/5/17 26/5/17	-	Battery carried on with R.E. fatigues by day and working parties in the line by night, ration parties for the detachments in the line, & ammunition carrying parties	D.H.I.

WAR DIARY or INTELLIGENCE SUMMARY

Army Form C. 2118.

Place	Date	Hour	Summary of Events and Information	Remarks and references to Appendices
ROYAULCOURT	27/5/17	-	2nd Lt D. NORMAN with a party of sixteen relieved 2nd Lt. LANDON in the line taking over the Guns and all spare parts	D.H.
do	28/5/17 to 30/5/17	-	Battery carried on Fatigues & work parties as before. 300 Rounds of Ammunition were prepared for firing, and carried forward to the line. The distance between our emplacements, and important enemy positions, was greater than the range of our Mortars, and it was impossible to engage them. German minenwerfer fired on our trenches, at a greater range, than that of our Mortars.	D.H.
do	31/5/17	-	Lt SAYERS with a party of sixteen, relieved 2nd Lt NORMAN in the line, taking over the Guns, and all spare parts, and, in addition, carrying up another Gun, making a total of four Mortars, in the line. Gun trenches and the ground in front, were reconnoitred by Capt HAWKES and Lt SAYERS with a view to engaging enemy targets from positions in no-man's-land, if necessary.	D.H.

D.H./Aycroft
127 T.M. Battery

127th Light Trench Mortar Battery

June to December 1917.

(6339) Wt. W160/M3016 1,500,000 10/17 McA & W Ltd (E1898) Forms W3091.

Army Form W.3091:

Cover for Documents.

———

Nature of Enclosures.

Operation File

175th Brigade
Orders

Notes, or Letters written.

58th (LONDON) DIVISION
-7 SEP. 1918
GENERAL STAFF

Confidential

War Diary
of
19th &
127th Light Trench Mortar Battery
from
June 1st to 30th 1917.

Vol. 1

WAR DIARY or INTELLIGENCE SUMMARY.

Army Form C. 2118.

(Erase heading not required.)

Place	Date	Hour	Summary of Events and Information	Remarks and references to Appendices
RUYAULCOURT	1/6/17	-	R/ccc, Sheet No.1, N.W. EUROPE (D5) We engaged enemy patrols & work parties with one Mortar, firing 60 rounds from our front line trench.	D.H.L.
	2/6/17	-	Preparing Ammunition in the line, and doing R.E. fatigues.	D.H.L.
	3/6/17	-	48 rounds were fired from one Mortar, from our front line trench on Enemy patrols.	D.H.L.
	4/6/17	-	2nd LIEUT LANDON with a party of sixteen, relieved LIEUT. SAYERS in the line	D.H.L.
	5/6/17	-	All available men, not in the line, proceeded to the line at 8 p.m. and worked on two new emplacements.	D.H.L.
	6/6/17	-	Party again went up to the line at 8 p.m to complete two new emplacements and to carry ammunition to them.	D.H.L.
	7/6/17	-	Party again proceeded to the line at 8.p.m and completed the work of carrying up 200 rounds to new emplacements and putting two Mortars in position (defensively)	D.H.L.
	8/6/17	-	Two new positions manned by detachments of five O.R's each, and four remaining Mortars put in temporary positions in the line to counteract, if necessary, any hostile attacks whilst the Brigade was digging a new ~~front~~ line	D.H.L.
	9/6/17	-	Eight Mortars were kept in position as in previous night	D.H.L.
	10/6/17	-	All Mortars were again kept in position and 69 rounds were fired from two, at hostile patrols and Machine Gun. 2nd LIEUT NORMAN and a party of sixteen relieved 2nd LIEUT LANDON in the line, four Mortars were withdrawn from the line to RUYAULCOURT	D.H.L.

WAR DIARY or INTELLIGENCE SUMMARY

Army Form C. 2118.

Place	Date	Hour	Summary of Events and Information	Remarks and references to Appendices
RUYAULCOURT	11/6/17 to 13/6/17	—	Ammunition was prepared for firing in the line, training was carried on at RUYAULCOURT for the part of the Battery on rest. One Mortar was withdrawn from a part of the line taken over by another Brigade.	D.H.S.
	14/6/17	—	LIEUT SAYERS with a party of sixteen, relieved the detachments in the line.	D.H.S.
	15/6/17 to 17/6/17	—	Battery training was carried on at RUYAULCOURT.	D.H.S.
	18/6/17	—	A party of sixteen under 2nd LIEUT LANDON relieved the detachments in the line.	D.H.S.
	19/6/17 to 21/6/17	—	Men not in the line, worked in HAVRINCOURT WOOD constructing new Battery headquarters.	D.H.S.
	22/6/17	—	A party of sixteen under 2nd LIEUT NORMAN relieved the detachments in the line.	D.H.S.
HAVRINCOURT WOOD	23/6/17	—	Battery Headquarters, opened here, at 4 p.m. (Ref Sheet No 1, N.W. EUROPE (O6)	D.H.S.
	24/6/17	—	One detachment of five, was moved from RUYAULCOURT to Battery H.Q in HAVRINCOURT WOOD.	D.H.S.
	25/6/17	—	Two Mortars gave a burst of fire for fifteen seconds on hostile working party, 21 rounds were fired.	D.H.S.
	26/6/17	—	LIEUT SAYERS with a party of sixteen relieved the detachments in the line. Two new defensive positions were occupied. The two mortars being carried forward from our old defensive positions, fifty fully prepared rounds were carried forward to each position.	D.H.S.
	28/6/17 to 29/6/17	—	300 rounds of ammunition were carried forward to the line and prepared for firing.	D.H.S.
	30/6/17	—	2nd LIEUT LANDON with a party of sixteen, relieved the detachments in the line.	D.H.S.

D.H.Sayers Lt.
127th T.M. Battery

Confidential
War Diary
of the
127th Light Trench Mortar Battery
From July 1st to July 31st 1917
Volume 1.

WAR DIARY or INTELLIGENCE SUMMARY

Army Form C. 2118.

(Erase heading not required.)

Place	Date	Hour	Summary of Events and Information	Remarks and references to Appendices
HAVRINCOURT WOOD	1/7/17	-	(Refe. Sheet No4, N.W. EUROPE, E5) Battery engaged preparing and carrying ammunition to positions in the front line	D.A.1
	2/7/17	-	All available men proceeded to the line and built eight emplacements, from which to fire on the night 2/3rd July. Forty rounds were carried to each emplacement and the Mortars placed in their positions after dark.	D.A.1
	3/7/17	-	At 1/8 a.m., in accordance with a raid, which was taking place a Barrage fire was opened by the eight Mortars, for 1 minute 45 seconds. The charge used was Green Cartridge, with one ring, and owing to the debris of the calico fabric of the rings, it was found impossible to maintain a consistent and rapid rate of fire for that time. 290 Bombs were fired in all, during the minute and 45 seconds.	D.A.1
	4/7/17	-	2nd Lt NORMAN with a party of sixteen relieved the detachments in the line	D.A.1
	5/7/17	-	Kit Inspection & Baths and cleaning up.	D.A.1
	6/7/17	-	120 Rounds were fired by three Mortars at suspected enemy working parties after dark	D.A.1
	7/7/17	-	Arrangements were completed for relief of the Battery by the 175th Trench Mortar Battery which was expected at 11.30 p.m.	D.A.1
	8/7/17	-	Relief completed at 3.30 a.m. owing to the difficulty experienced by 175th Trench Mortar Battery in bringing up their guns spare base plates & various equipment to the Gun positions. Much trouble would	D.A.1

WAR DIARY or INTELLIGENCE SUMMARY

Army Form C. 2118.

Place	Date	Hour	Summary of Events and Information	Remarks and references to Appendices
HAVRINCOURT WOOD	8/7/17	-	have been saved, if Guns had been exchanged. Battery Headquarters moved back to RUYAULCOURT (Rfce, Sheet No 4, N.W. EUROPE, D5)	D.16/1
BARASTRE	9/7/17	-	Battery trekked to BARASTRE (Rfce, Sheet No 4, N.W. EUROPE, D5). Time of Departure 2.40 p.m., arrived at destination 4 p.m. Transport provided - Stores, with the exception of Guns and Ammunition, were sent on ahead to ACHIET-LE-GRAND (Rfce, Sheet No 4, N.W. EUROPE, C.4) by rail. Guns and Ammunition (210 Rounds) were carried by one G.S. Limbered Wagon, and one G.S. Wagon along with the Battery.	D.16/1
ACHIET	10/7/17	-	(Rfce, Sheet No 4, N.W. EUROPE, C.4.) Battery moved with the Brigade to ACHIET; time of Departure 8.40 a.m., Arriving at destination at 2.p.m. Transport provided - as for previous day.	D.16/1
	11/7/17 to 31/7/17		Battery training carried on. Six hours of training done per day. Training was of a progressive nature, starting with Gun Instruction and Drill, then digging in and ranging, then tactical work and live firing. Squad Drill, Musketry, Gas Drill, and Physical Training were also carried out each day. Baths were made frequent use of and sometimes was set apart for various sports. Battery was re-organized & re-equipped to the necessary extent.	D.16/1

D.H. Ayerst
127th F.T. Battery

Confidential
War Diary
of the
10th Light Trench Mortar Battery
for August 1917
Volume 1.

WAR DIARY or INTELLIGENCE SUMMARY.

Army Form C. 2118.

(Erase heading not required.)

Instructions regarding War Diaries and Intelligence Summaries are contained in F. S. Regs., Part II. and the Staff Manual respectively. Title pages will be prepared in manuscript.

Place	Date	Hour	Summary of Events and Information	Remarks and references to Appendices
ACHIET LE ~~PETIT~~	1/8/17 to 20/8/17	-	(Refce N.W. EUROPE, SHEET No 4, C4) Battery trainings carried on including Musketry, Bayonet fighting, and Gas Drill. Full use was made of the Divisional Baths. Time was set apart for Route Marches and Sports. The Battery participated in two Brigade tactical offensive schemes.	DHA
AVELUY	21/8/17	-	(Refce N.W. EUROPE Sheet no 4, B5) The Battery moved with Brigade from ACHIET to AVELUY. Moved off 8-45 a.m. arrived at destination 1 p.m. Transport provided, - one G.S. Wagon and one G.S. Limbered Wagon for Mortars and Ammunition. One Motor Wagon for Battery Stores.	DHA
POPERINGHE	22/8/17	-	(Refce N.W. EUROPE Sheet 1 and part of 4) Battery moved by rail to Billets near POPERINGHE. Moved off at 7 a.m. Entrained at 9-45 a.m. Detrained at HOPOUTRE sidings, POPERINGHE at 10-30 p.m. arrived at destination at 11-30 p.m. Stores, Handcarts and Mobile reserve consisting of two Mortars and 110 rounds of Ammunition were carried on the same train. The remaining six Mortars were carried with the Divisional Ammunition Column on a later train.	DHA
do	23/8/17 to 30/8/17	-	Training carried on. Formations when advancing, and positions in the attack being practised	DHA
do	31/8/17	-	Battery moved to Hutments between POPERINGHE and VLAMERTINGHE. Moved off at 7 a.m. Arrived at destination 9-45 a.m. Transport provided - One G.S. Wagon for Mobile reserve, One Motor Wagon for Battery Stores, Baggage and remaining six Mortars. Day was spent in cleaning and tidying Billets.	DHA

D H Sayers /-

Confidential
War Diary
of the
1st Trench Mortar Battery
from Sept 1st 1917
to
Sept 30th 1917
Volume 1.

WAR DIARY
or
INTELLIGENCE SUMMARY.

(Erase heading not required.)

Army Form C. 2118.

Instructions regarding War Diaries and Intelligence Summaries are contained in F. S. Regs., Part II. and the Staff Manual respectively. Title pages will be prepared in manuscript.

Place	Date	Hour	Summary of Events and Information	Remarks and references to Appendices
POPERINGHE	1/9/17 to 6/9/17		(Ref. N.W. Europe sheet 1 & part of 4. C.8.) Battery training carried on.	D&1
YPRES D.8.	7/9/17		Battery relieved the 125th French Mortar Battery in the line, East of YPRES, (Ref. D.8) Two Officers and 35 O.R's, took over in the line. Seven Mortars were taken up, but none put in position. One Officer and remainder of the Battery, proceeded to Brigade Rear Head Quarters, near YPRES (D.8) as a battle surplus. Transport provided – Three G.S. Wagons.	D&1
do	8/9/17		The Brigade front was reconnoitred, with a view to finding suitable emplacements for Stokes Mortars.	D&1
do	9/9/17		After dark, parties went up to the front line, and commenced digging emplacements at positions, which had been chosen the previous night.	D&1
do	10/9/17		The Officer at Brigade Rear Head Quarters, proceeded to the line, as, in view of the tactical situation which would arise during our imminent offensive, two Officers would be insufficient to control the Battery in the line. During the night, work was carried on at the pits, and a carrying party of 120 carried 350 rounds of ammunition to the pits. Plans, formulated before, were completed in detail, for the tactical use of our men, and mortars, to the best advantage during the attack, and especially in case of counter attack: ranging would be effected by bursts of rapid fire during our barrage; the men would then be in readiness to open rapid fire at any time, covering the ground on which, the enemy must assemble for his counter attack. On the right front of the attack, one Officer	D&1

WAR DIARY or INTELLIGENCE SUMMARY.

Army Form C. 2118.

(Erase heading not required.)

Place	Date	Hour	Summary of Events and Information	Remarks and references to Appendices
YPRES (D.8.)	10/9/17	-	would be in charge of 4 mortars; on the left, another would be in charge of 3. The details of fire control arranged were simple and ample.	DAS.
do	11/9/17	-	The offensive, for which preparation had been made, was cancelled.	DAS.
do	12/9/17	-	The battle surplus of the Battery, which had stayed at Brigade Rear Head Quarters, was ordered to the line.	DAS.
do	13/9/17	-	The entire Battery was engaged digging jumping-off trenches, during the night 13th/14th.	DAS.
do	14/9/17	-	Battery was engaged by fatigues, & preparation for relief.	DAS.
POPERINGHE (C.8.)	15/9/17	-	The Battery was relieved by the 125th Trench Mortar Battery. Relief was completed at 12·30 a.m. Total casualties whilst in the line for these seven days, — 5 O.R's wounded. Battery proceeded to hutments, between POPERINGHE (C.8.) and VLAMERTINGHE (C.8.) by rail arriving at hutments at 4·30 a.m. Transport provided,— 3 G.S Wagons. One Officer and all available O.R's proceeded as a work party to dig cable trenches, and bury cables, East of YPRES (D.8.)	DAS.
do	16/9/17	-	One Officer and all available O.R's proceeded, as a work party, for duty as on previous night.	DAS.
do	17/9/17	-	Battery moved to another Camp near POPERINGHE (C.8.). Transport provided, one motor lorry and one limber. Battery moved off at 3·30 p.m. and arrived at destination at 4·30 p.m.	DAS.
~~do~~	19/9/17	-	Battery moved to another Camp in the vicinity of POPERINGHE (C.8.)	DAS.

WAR DIARY or INTELLIGENCE SUMMARY

Army Form C. 2118.

Place	Date	Hour	Summary of Events and Information	Remarks and references to Appendices
WINNEZEELE (B.8.)	20/9/17	.	Battery moved to Billets at WINNEZEELE (Rfee B.8.). Time of departure, - 7 a.m, time of arrival, - 1 p.m. Transport provided was 1 Motor lorry. A loading party of 1 N.C.O and 3 O.R's was left behind to load motor lorry when it should arrive.	DAS
do	21/9/17	.	Battery transport - i.e. 11 handcarts joined Brigade Transport and was taken forward to WORMHOUDT (Rfee A.8.) by 1 Officer & personnel of Battery. Time of departure, - 1.30 p.m. Time of arrival at WORMHOUDT (A.8.) - 6.30 p.m. Motor lorry, with stores, baggage, & guns which were left with loading party at POPERINGHE (C.8.) arrived at WINNEZEELE (B.8.) at 4.30 p.m.	DAS
COXYDE (B.6.)	22/9/17	.	Battery Head Quarters moved to COXYDE (B.6.) by bus. Transport provided;- half a motor lorry. There was insufficient room for our authorised stores on the half lorry, so 2 men were left as a guard (loading party) over the stores, which it was necessary to leave behind. The Officer & party with the handcarts, proceeded with Brigade Transport, from WORMHOUDT (A.8.) to COXYDE (B.6.) It was found impossible, for the men to pull the handcarts, & keep up with Brigade Transport, after more than ten miles. Thereafter the handcarts were placed on empty supply wagons of the train & the party marched on in fatigue dress. Time of departure from WORMHOUDT (A.8.); 10.30 a.m. Time of arrival at Canada Camp, COXYDE (B.6.); 11.30 p.m.	DAS
do	24/9/17	.	One Officer & 23 O.R's moved off at 9 p.m, to relieve the 199th Trench Mortar Battery in the line at NIEUPORT. BAINS (C.5.)	DAS

WAR DIARY or INTELLIGENCE SUMMARY.

Army Form C. 2118.

(Erase heading not required.)

Place	Date	Hour	Summary of Events and Information	Remarks and references to Appendices
COXYDE (B.6.)	25/9/17	-	Relief completed in the line at 2 a.m. 8 Mortars were taken over. 4 of these were in position, laid on enemy targets. The other 4 were in reserve at Head Quarters in the line. In exchange, we handed over 8 mortars, at Battery Rear Head Quarters. Head Quarters & the remainder of the Battery moved to Surrey Camp at 1-15 a.m. arriving at 2-15 a.m. Transport provided, - 1 G.S. Wagon & 1 Limber.	D.A.1.
do	26/9/17	-	The Battery stores that were left at WINNEZEELE (B.8.) on 22/9/17 arrived by motor lorry.	D.A.1.
do	27/9/17	-	In the line, our 4 mortars were re-registered on their respective zero lines, 50 rounds were fired on enemy targets, during the day. In retaliation to Trench Mortar fire, on our infantry, 30 rounds were fired in early morning on a point, where new enemy work, had been observed in progress.	D.A.1.
do	28/9/17	-	The position from which the enemy Trench Mortar appeared to fire, was registered by one of our Mortars.	D.A.1.
do	29/9/17	-	In early morning the enemy Trench Mortar opened fire twice, & was engaged by our Mortar, 60 rounds being fired by us. On each occasion the enemy Trench Mortar ceased firing when we opened.	D.A.1.
do	30/9/17	-	At 3-30 p.m. we fired on enemy targets, in conjunction with Artillery & medium mortars. Damage was done to enemy wire, & works. In retaliation to enemy Trench Mortar fire, on our trenches during the night, a further 40 rounds were fired on the works, which we damaged during the day.	D.A.1.

Confidential
War Diary
of the
127th Light Trench Mortar Battery
from
October 1st 1917
to
October 31st 1917.

Volume 1

Map BELGIUM
Sheets 11 & 12.

WAR DIARY
and
INTELLIGENCE SUMMARY.
(Erase heading not required.)

Army Form C. 2118.
127th Lt Trench Mortar Battery. Sheet 1.

Place	Date	Hour	Summary of Events and Information	Remarks and references to Appendices
COXYDE	1/10/17	—	(Rfce.- N.W. Europe. Sheets and part of 4. B.6.) A party of one Officer and 23 O.Rs. relieved the party of the Battery in the line at NIEUPORT BAINS (Rfce. - C.5)	DW/
-Do-	2/10/17 to 5/10/17	—	The party in the line at NIEUPORT BAINS (Rfce.- C.5.) continued the policy of firing our four mortars on enemy infantry and works in retaliation of his firing on our infantry and works. Shoots were also arranged in conjunction with our Artillery, & heavy and medium trench mortars; good destructive results were observed.	DW/
-Do-	6/10/17	—	The Battery was relieved by the 123rd Trench Mortar Battery. The relief was complete by midnight. Battery Headquarters moved to new billets at COXYDE- BAINS (B.6.)	DW/
-Do-	7/10/17	—	The Battery moved to CANADA CAMP, near COXYDE (B.6.) Hour of departure from COXYDE BAINS, - 11.15 A.M., hour of arrival at destination - 12.15 p.m.. The transport provided was one G.S. limbered wagon; this made four journeys, and the remainder of the Battery stores and baggage was carried by journeys with hand carts.	DW/
-Do-	8/10/17 to 21/10/17	—	Battery training was carried on. In addition the Battery was engaged by R.E. fatigues. The line at NIEUPORT	DW/

WAR DIARY
INTELLIGENCE SUMMARY.
(Erase heading not required.)

Army Form C. 2118.

127th Lt Trench Mortar Battery. Sheet 1-2

Place	Date	Hour	Summary of Events and Information	Remarks and references to Appendices
COXYDE	8/10/17 to 21/10/17	-	NIEUPORT and LOMBARTZIDE (C.5.) was reconnoitred with a view to relieving the 125th Trench Mortar Battery.	DHS
NIEUPORT	22/10/17	-	The Battery relieved the 125th Trench Mortar Battery in the line east of NIEUPORT (C.6.) The relief was complete at 9 p.m. Battery Headquarters was established at NIEUPORT (C.6.) We exchanged seven mortars with the 125th Battery. This obviated the necessity, otherwise, of carrying them to and from their positions in the line. Three mortars were in position to be used offensively or defensively; three in position to be used defensively only (i.e., in the case of our front line falling into enemy hands) and two were held in reserve.	DHS
Do.	23/10/17 to 31/10/17	-	A policy of only firing at night, and then only in retaliation to enemy Minenwerfer fire, was maintained. The Company Commanders in charge of the line where our mortars were placed, ~~was~~ ~~asked to~~ agreed to ask for retaliation from us when they required it. The N.C.Os. in charge of each gun were also instructed to fire immediately on enemy minenwerfer opening on our front system. A	DHS

WAR DIARY
INTELLIGENCE SUMMARY.

127th T. Trench Mortar Battery Sheet 3.

Army Form C. 2118.

Place	Date	Hour	Summary of Events and Information	Remarks and references to Appendices
Nieuport	23/10/17 to 31/10/17		A few rounds were fired. Of the three mortars in defensive positions, two were put into positions available for offensive use as well as defensive. All the positions are greatly improved. D.A.S Ayers Lt	D.A.S

Confidential

War Diary
of the
121st Light Trench Mortar Battery
from
November 1st 1917
to
November 30th 1917

Volume 2.

WAR DIARY or INTELLIGENCE SUMMARY.

Army Form C. 2118.

(Erase heading not required.)

Place	Date	Hour	Summary of Events and Information	Remarks and references to Appendices
			(Area N.W. EUROPE	
NIEUPORT (C.6.)	1/11/17 to 6/11/17	-	A few rounds (work) fired in retaliation. Much work was done on improving the existing emplacements and two new offensive emplacements were constructed.	S/1.
to	7/11/17	-	The Battery was relieved by the 125th L.T.M.Bty. Relief completed by 9 p.m. Battery left NIEUPORT at 9.30 p.m. arriving at CANADA CAMP (B.6) at 12 midnight. Transport provided one limber.	S/1.
CANADA CAMP (B.6)	8/11/17 to 15/11/17	-	Battery training was carried out. In addition the Battery was engaged by fatigues in NIEUPORT.	S/1.
to	16/11/17	-	Relieved by the French, the battery entrained at COXYDE (B.6) at 12-30 p.m. arriving at LEFFRINCKOUCKE (A.6) at 2-45 p.m. and in billets by 4 p.m. Six handcarts accompanied us, the remainder were left at ST IDESBALDE (B.6) under a guard to come by rail.	S/1.
LEFFRINCKOUCKE (A.6)	17/11/17	-	Battery left LEFFRINCKOUCKE (A.6) at 9 a.m arriving at WORMHOUDT (A.8) 5-45 p.m	S/1.
WORMHOUDT (A.8)	18/11/17	-	The march continued, leaving WORMHOUDT (A.8) at 8-45 a.m arriving at RIETVELD (A.8) at 10 a.m.	S/1.
RIETVELD	19/11/17	-	Battery left RIETVELD (A8) at 9-30 am arriving at OXELEARE (A9) at 1 p.m.	S/1.

WAR DIARY or INTELLIGENCE SUMMARY.

Army Form C. 2118.

(Erase heading not required.)

Instructions regarding War Diaries and Intelligence Summaries are contained in F. S. Regs., Part II. and the Staff Manual respectively. Title pages will be prepared in manuscript.

Place	Date	Hour	Summary of Events and Information	Remarks and references to Appendices
OXELEARE (A.9.)	20/11/17	-	Battery marched from OXELEARE (A.9.) at 9·30 a.m. arriving at BERGUETTE (A.10.) at 4·30 p.m. During this march and on the 17th inst arrangements were made for a mid-day meal en-route. One Motor Lorry was provided to carry Guns, Stores etc. the whole journey. The handcarts left to come by rail arrived at BERGUETTE STATION.	S/1.
BERGUETTE (A.10.)	21/11/17 to 25/11/17	-	Battery training was continued	S/1.
do	26/11/17		Battery marched from BERGUETTE to VENDIN (B.11.) arriving there at 3·15 p.m. Transport provided one Motor Lorry. Lt SAYERS went in advance to reconnoitre the sector about to be taken over by us.	S/1.
VENDIN (B.11)	27/11/17		Battery relieved the 7th L.T.M. Bty in the GIVENCHY sector (C.11.) guides were met at GORRE (Battery rear Head Quarters) at 2·30 p.m. LT SAYERS & party relieved the three Guns in left sub-sector and LT LANDON and party relieved the five Guns in the right sub-sector. Relief complete by 6·30 p.m when Battery Head Quarters opened at FESTUBERT (C.11.). Transport provided for the move two G.S. Wagons.	S/1.

WAR DIARY
or
INTELLIGENCE SUMMARY.
(Erase heading not required.)

Army Form C. 2118.

Place	Date	Hour	Summary of Events and Information	Remarks and references to Appendices
GIVENCHY (C.11.)	28/11/17	-	Several rounds were fired during the day in retaliation to hostile T.M. fire all Guns having been carefully checked and registered	S/1.
do	29/11/17	-	A small shoot was carried out successfully in conjunction with the Medium Trench Mortars in retaliation	S/1.
do	30/11/17	-	Our Mortars fired occasionally in retaliation, considerable work was done on strengthening & improving our emplacements.	S/1.

H. Jenkins Captn
O/c Battery.

Confidential
War Diary
of the
107th Light Trench Mortar Battery
from
December 1st/1917
to
December 31st/1917
Volume 1.

WAR DIARY or INTELLIGENCE SUMMARY.

Army Form C. 2118.

(Erase heading not required.)

Place	Date	Hour	Summary of Events and Information	Remarks and references to Appendices
FESTUBERT (C.11.)	1/12/17 to 22/12/17		(Reference, N.W. Europe, Sheet 1 & part of 4. C.11.) Fire, to the extent of an average of 120 rounds per day. was maintained on the enemy front and support lines. Firing was invariably carried out immediately on the enemy T.M's. becoming active, and as a rule the activity of the latter immediately subsided on our mortars opening fire. In addition, two successful shoots were carried out by single mortars firing rapid on enemy M.Gs. the positions of which had been accurately located. These shoots were done in conjunction with the ~~Company~~ Lewis Guns. of the Company holding the Sector. Observation was easy on this front and direct hits on trenches and works and damage done was often observed.	D.O.I.
Do.	22/12/17		The Battery was relieved by the 125th Trench Mortar Battery, Relief was complete at 2 p.m. The Battery marched to BETHUNE (Ref. B.11.) arriving at 3.30 p.m. Transport provided, - one motor lorry.	D.O.I.
BETHUNE	22/12/17 to 29/12/17		Battery training was carried on in accordance with	D.O.I.

Place	Date	Hour	Summary of Events and Information	Remarks and references to Appendices
BETHUNE	22/12/17 to 28/12/17		with S.S. 152, and S.S. 143 & S.S. 137. Christmas Day was celebrated by a holiday, Church service, dinner & festivities. The Battery moved to OBLINGHEM (Rfce B.11.) Transport provided,- 1 motor lorry.	DAS
OBLINGHEM	28/12/17 to 31/12/17		(Rfce N.W. Europe Sheet 1 & part of 4, B.11.) Battery training carried on.	DAS

DAS Curush

Confidential.

War Diary.

of

127th Light Trench Mortar Bty.

For Jan. 1918.

Vol. II.

WAR DIARY of INTELLIGENCE SUMMARY.

Army Form C. 2118.

(Erase heading not required.)

Place	Date	Hour	Summary of Events and Information	Remarks and references to Appendices
OBLINGHEM	1/1/18 to 3/1/18		Reference – N.W. EUROPE, Sheet I and part of IV. (Rfce B.13.) Battery training carried on in accordance with S.S.152, S.S.143 and S.S.137. The trenches in the LA BASSEE CANAL and CUINCHY sector (Rfce C.11.) were reconnoitred on account of an impending relief.	DH1
BEUVRY	3/1/18		(Rfce C.11.) The Battery relieved the 126th L.T.M. Battery in the line at CUINCHY, Battery H.Q. being established near BEUVRY (Rfce C.11.) Transport provided for the move was one motor lorry. Seven mortars were taken over in the line in firing positions and one mortar to be held in reserve at ~~H.Q.~~ Battery H.Q. The mortars in the line were in offensive positions.	DH1
Do.	4/1/18 to 29/1/18		During this period our mortars were actively engaged in replying to, and in some cases, in neutralising enemy T.M. fire. An average of ninety rounds was fired each day. Enemy light T.M's. remained very quiet; in most cases his heavy T.M's. fired from beyond our range. Our retaliation to his light T.M's. was five to one. On several occasions our gun pits were damaged by hostile T.M. and shell fire. Adverse weather conditions also damaged the pits and R.E. assistance in addition to the	DH1

WAR DIARY or INTELLIGENCE SUMMARY

Army Form C. 2118.

(Erase heading not required.)

Place	Date	Hour	Summary of Events and Information	Remarks and references to Appendices
BEUVRY	4/1/18 to 29/1/18		Reference N.W. EUROPE Sheet I and part of IV. (Ptce C.11.) The work of all our own spare men was required to keep our positions in a state of repair. Infantry carrying parties of ten O.Rs were supplied us each day and carried ammunition from the Brigade Ammunition Dump direct to the gun positions.	D.S.
Do.	29/1/18		The Battery was relieved by the 125th L.T.M. Battery. Battery moved to billets in BEUVRY. Transport provided for the move, - three G.S. Waggons.	D.S.
Do.	30/1/18		Kit inspections were carried out and general cleaning up done.	D.S.
	31/1/18		Fatigue party of one Officer and 25 O.Rs. was furnished. Remainder of the Battery was occupied by doing various fatigues in connection with billets, cook houses and latrines.	D.S.

D. S. Carver Lt.

Confidential

War Diary

of the

134th Light Trench Mortar Battery

from

February 1st/1918
to
February 28th/1918

Volume 1.

WAR DIARY or INTELLIGENCE SUMMARY.

(Erase heading not required.)

Army Form C. 2118.

Place	Date	Hour	Summary of Events and Information	Remarks and references to Appendices
BEUVRY	1/2/18 to 12/2/18		Rfce - N.W. EUROPE, Sheet 1 & part of 4 (Rfce C.11.) A daily party of One Officer and 25 O.R's was supplied for R.E. work. Remainder of the Battery carried on simple training.	DA1
BURBURE	12/2/18		(Rfce A.11.) Battery was relieved by 165th T.M.Battery. Battery left BEUVRY at 6-30 a.m. marching with handcarts and arrived at BURBURE at 12.30 p.m. Transport provided was One Motor lorry.	DA1
do	13/2/18 to 28/2/18		Progressive training was carried out in accordance with the latest manuals of instruction. The subjects of training included all Infantry exercises and special training in Trench Mortar work, including Map reading and use of the Compass, Gun Instruction and drill, registration work, live firing & framing of reports. An experimental practise of Anti-aircraft fire was also carried out with some benefit and success. Douglas A. Sayers Lt	DA1

127th LIGHT TRENCH MORTAR BATTERY

MARCH 1918

42nd Division.
127th Infantry Brigade.

WAR DIARY or INTELLIGENCE SUMMARY.

(Erase heading not required.)

Army Form C. 2118.

Instructions regarding War Diaries and Intelligence Summaries are contained in F. S. Regs., Part II. and the Staff Manual respectively. Title pages will be prepared in manuscript.

Place	Date	Hour	Summary of Events and Information	Remarks and references to Appendices
BURBURE 36a S.W. 1/20000	1/3/18 to 4/3/18		Battery training and anti-aircraft practices carried on.	DA1
BUSNES 36a S.E. 1/20,000	4/3/18		Battery left BURBURE at 1.30 p.m. and arrived at LE PIRE near BUSNES at 3 p.m. Transport provided, — One motor lorry.	DA1
Do.	4/3/18 to 23/3/18		Battery training and anti-aircraft practices carried on.	DA1
Do.	23/3/18		Embussed in motor lorries at 12.30 p.m. Five hand-carts and Battery Stores for which there was no room were left behind at the Brigade Dump at BUSNES with a guard of two men.	DA1
AYETTE 51D 1/40,000	24/3/18		(Reference LENS 11. Ed.2. 1/100000, I.4.) Arrived at COURCELLES Aerodrome near AYETTE (I.4.) at 1.30 a.m. Officer's valises, mess stores & Battery baggage were left there, with Battle Supplies. At 8.45 p.m. the Battery marched with six hand carts to GOMIECOURT (J. 5.)	DA1
GOMIECOURT	25/3/18		(Ref. J.5.) Battery arrived at GOMIECOURT at 12.30 a.m. Meantime an enemy attack had developed on our front at MORY (K5) and on either flank. Approximately 100 stragglers of various units and Divisions were collected and acting	DA1

WAR DIARY or INTELLIGENCE SUMMARY.

Army Form C. 2118.

(Erase heading not required.)

Place	Date	Hour	Summary of Events and Information	Remarks and references to Appendices
GOMMECOURT	25/3/18		(Rte J.5.) acting under the orders of a Brigadier General of the 40th Division a position was taken up North of GOMMECOURT where the party (about 150 strong) dug themselves in and was prepared to act in support of the infantry in front. When the situation cleared somewhat at 4 a.m. orders were received to proceed to GOMMECOURT and remain there. The Battery did this, the stragglers collected being taken over by an Officer of the 40th Division. During the day good work was done by 2/Lt NORMAN (4th York & Lancs) and Lt HACKER (7th Manchesters) both attached 127th T.M.B. in collecting and carrying S.A.A. under heavy shell fire to the 6th Manchesters. Enemy attacks again developed and the Battery acting under the orders of a Staff Colonel of the 40th Division R.A., took up positions West of GOMMECOURT in support of the infantry in front, and after dusk withdrew along with other units to trenches in LOGEAST Wood (J.5.) The Battery guns had been left in force at GOMMECOURT (J.5.)	D.H.
ABLAINZEVELLE	26/3/18		At 3 a.m. Lt SAYERS (7th Res S.R.) attached 127th T.M.B. with all available men of the Battery & some stragglers of the 8th Manchesters re-entered GOMMECOURT and withdrew the guns, with some difficulty owing to rifle & M.G. fire	D.H.

WAR DIARY or INTELLIGENCE SUMMARY.

Army Form C. 2118.

(Erase heading not required.)

Place	Date	Hour	Summary of Events and Information	Remarks and references to Appendices
ABLAINZEVELLE	26/3/18		(Rfce J.5.) At 3.30 a.m. the Battery withdrew to ABLAINZEVELLE (J.5.) Battery withdrew from ABLAINZEVELLE (J.5.) at 10.30 a.m. carrying the guns on the three remaining handcarts.	DAA
FONQUEVILLERS	26/3/18		(Rfce H.5.) Battery arrived here at 9.30 p.m. and at once got into touch with 42nd Divisional H.Q. where orders were received to stand by until instructions from our Brigade were received.	DAA
Do.	27/3/18		Battery remained at FONQUEVILLERS (H.5.) in accordance with orders from Brigade. The line at Bucquoy (J.5.) was reconnoitred.	DAA
ESSARTS le Bucquoy	28/3/18		(Rfce J.5.) Battery moved to ESSARTS le Bucquoy (J.5.) arriving here at 5 p.m. All guns were sent to the Brigade Transport lines with two men to look after them. The Battle Surplus rejoined the Battery.	DAA
Do.	29/3/18		The Battery remained in reserve at ESSARTS le Bucquoy (J.5.)	DAA
Do.	30/3/18		The Battery moved at 10 p.m. to trenches between GOMMECOURT (H.5.) and FONQUEVILLERS (H.5.) arriving here at midnight.	DAA

D A S Curush L

127th LIGHT TRENCH MORTAR BATTERY.

A P R I L

1 9 1 8

127th Inf. Bde.
42nd Div.

Confidential

War Diary
of the
129th Light-Armed Mortar Battery
from
April 1st 1918
to
April 30th 1918

Volume 2.

Instructions regarding War Diaries and Intelligence Summaries are contained in F. S. Regs., Part II. and the Staff Manual respectively. Title pages will be prepared in manuscript.

INTELLIGENCE SUMMARY.
(Erase heading not required.)

Place	Date	Hour	Summary of Events and Information (Refer LENS 11 ED 2 1/100,000)	Remarks and references to Appendices
ESSARTS LE BUCQUOY	1/4/18		Battery moved to ESSARTS LE BUCQUOY (J.5.) arriving here at 9.15 pm	
	2/4/18		The Battery remained at ESSARTS (J.5.)	
	3/4/18		At 8 a.m. Battery moved into dug-outs in old German line West of Pigeon Wood.	R.H.
ABLAINZEVILLE (J.5.)	4/4/18		Battery relieved 126" L.T.M.B. in the line at ABLAINZEVILLE (J.5.) LT SAYERS & LT HACKER and party took over four guns on the 1/6 M/cr sector. BATTERY H.Q. at ESSARTS (J.5.) During the night 4/5" the enemy heavily bombarded ESSARTS (J.5.) with Gas shells & H.E. Battery suffered about twenty casualties (including 2nd LT LANDON 1/10th M.P.) from the effects of the Gas.	R.H.
	5/4/18		Battery engaged aircraft & succeeded in bringing down one E.A. It also engaged enemy machine-guns with good effect.	
	6/4/18		Battery was relieved by the 176" L.T.M.B. at 11.30pm & marched	R.H.
	7/4/18		to SOUASTRE (S.5.) arriving here at 4 A.M on the 7th.	
	8/4/18		The Battery entrained at SOUASTRE (S.5.) at 4.30 a.m. and proceeded to LOUVENCOURT (F.5.) arriving here at 6 a.m	
LOUVENCOURT (F.5.)	9/4/18		Battery re-equipping, cleaning, reorganizing, & training.	
	15/4/18		Various lines of defence were reconnoitred by Capt HAWKES (2nd Royal BERKS)	R.H.

INTELLIGENCE SUMMARY.

(Erase heading not required.)

Place	Date	Hour	Summary of Events and Information	Remarks and references to Appendices
LOUVENCOURT	14.4.18		and Lieut SAYERS (5th Reserve S.R.) in (C.5)	RM
-do-	15.4.18 16.4.18		Battery relieved the 111th L.T.M.B. in the line at HEBUTERNE (H.5.) leaving LOUVENCOURT at 4.30pm & arriving at HEBUTERNE at 9pm. LT HACKER (16th Manchesters) and party took over four guns in the line. Battery H.Q. at HEBUTERNE (H.5.)	RM
HEBUTERNE	17.4.18		Battery received orders to take up defensive positions West of HEBUTERNE coming under direct orders of O.C. 16 Manchesters. Four guns in the line were withdrawn. LT HACKER (16th Manchesters) with two guns took up a position south west of HEBUTERNE and 2nd LT MAWSON (3rd Manchesters) with two guns took up a position north west of HEBUTERNE, two guns being kept in reserve. Position remained the same until the 19th.	RM
-do-	19.4.18		LT HACKER (16th Manchesters) & party took two guns into the line of the 16th Manchesters whilst 2nd LT MAWSON (3rd Manchesters) & party with two guns took up a fresh position in the centre of HEBUTERNE, & two guns in reserve being mounted for Anti-Aircraft work.	RM

INTELLIGENCE SUMMARY.

(Erase heading not required.)

Place	Date	Hour	Summary of Events and Information	Remarks and references to Appendices
HEBUTERNE	20.4.18 to 23.4.18		Position remained the same, bad conditions & poor observation prevented much firing. On the night of 22nd/23rd Capt HAWKES (2nd Royal Berks) & a party took up one gun into the line to support a raid, carried out at 2.30 a.m. by 1/6th Manchesters, firing about 50 rounds with good effect.	R.H.
do	24.4.18		Battery was relieved by the 1st N.Z. L.T.M.B. leaving HEBUTERNE at 6 p.m. going into billets at BAYENCOURT (G.5.) and arriving there at 8.30 p.m.	R.H.
BAYENCOURT	25.4.18 to 28.4.18		Cleaning, reorganising & training was carried out. Battery relieved the 125th L.T.M.B. in the line at SOMMECOURT (G.5) leaving BAYENCOURT at 7.45 p.m. arriving SOMMECOURT at 10 p.m. Battery H.Q. at SOMMECOURT. (G.5)	R.H.
SOMMECOURT	29.4.18 to 30.4.18		Fair amount of firing carried on in the line with good results.	R.H.

R. Heathcote-Hacker
2/Lt

Confidential

War Diary

of the

121st Light Trench Mortar Battery

from

1st May 1918
to
31st May 1918

Volume 2

WAR DIARY

Army Form C. 2118.

(Erase heading not required.)

Place	Date	Hour	Summary of Events and Information	Remarks and references to Appendices
			Reference, LENS. 11 EDITION. 2.	
SOMMECOURT H.5.	1-5-18 to 3-5-18	-	Retaliation fire, directed on enemy infantry targets, was carried on. Preparations were made to support, by a barrage, Brigade advance EAST of HEBUTERNE. (H.5.) to take place on 4-5-18.	R.A.
do	4-5-18	-	At 9.50 p.m. over 200 shells were fired on the enemy's lines EAST of HEBUTERNE (H.5.) prior to the 1/5th M/Cs relements of 1st N.Z. BRIGADE pushing forward our line at this point. After the raid the personnel of the four Guns, which had been in action, helped to clear the wounded to the dressing station.	R.A.
do	5-5-18	-	The Battery was relieved in the line by the 172nd L.T.M.B. Battery left SOMMECOURT (H.5.) at 10-30 p.m. and marched to HENU (D.5.) arriving there at 12.30 a.m. 6-5-18.	R.A.
HENU D.19.	6-5-18 to 4-5-18	-	Battery in billets in HENU (D.5). During this time Battery was engaged in keen training, including Tactical exercises carried out by the whole Brigade, for the defence of various lines of resistance in the FONQUEVILLERS area (H.5.)	R.A.

R. Heathcote Hartley

WAR DIARY ~~INTELLIGENCE SUMMARY~~

(Erase heading not required.)

Army Form C. 2118.

Instructions regarding War Diaries and Intelligence Summaries are contained in F. S. Regs., Part II. and the Staff Manual respectively. Title pages will be prepared in manuscript.

Ref. France. Sheet 57D ~~Edition~~ 2.

Place	Date	Hour	Summary of Events and Information	Remarks and references to Appendices
HENU	1-6-18 to 5-6-18	—	Battery in Billets in HENU (D.19.) During this time the Battery was engaged in keen training & re-organizing prior to going into the line.	
HEBUTERNE	6-6-18	—	Battery relieved the 1st N.Z.T.M.B. in the line at HEBUTERNE (K.10. & 16.) Battery H.Q. (K.9.c.) Battery left HENU (D.9.) at 10.30am arriving HEBUTERNE (K.9.) at 12.30pm. Relief complete at 4pm. Lieut HELCH, 1st K.O.R.L.R. took over in the line with 4 guns.	
—	7-6-18 to 13-6-18	—	Harrassing fire was carried on, on the enemys trench system with good effect and a number of destructive shoots were also carried out in conjunction with the Artillery & Medium Trench Mortars.	
—	14-6-18	—	Battery was relieved by the 125th T.M.B. Relief complete at 2.15 pm. Battery left HEBUTERNE (K.9.) at 2.30pm & marched to BUS WOODS (J.20.) arriving there at 4pm.	
BUS WOODS	15-6-18 to 22-6-18	—	Battery in Divisional Reserve in BUS WOODS (J.20.) under canvass. During this period Battery was engaged in cleaning up, improving the Camp, & Recreational Training.	

WAR DIARY or INTELLIGENCE SUMMARY.

Army Form C. 2118.

(Erase heading not required.)

Place	Date	Hour	Summary of Events and Information	Remarks and references to Appendices
			Ref. France Sheet 57.D. Edition 2.	
BUS WOODS.	23-6-18	—	Battery relieved 126th T.M.B. in the line in the Right Sub-Sector. Battery H.Q. at (J.24.d.) Battery left BUS WOODS (J.20) at 11am. arriving at new Battery H.Q. at 12.30pm. Relief complete at 3.30pm. 2/Lt. WYNNE Manchester Regt took over in the line with 6 guns.	R.T.D.
IN THE LINE.	24-1-18 to 30-1-18.	—	Harrassing fire was carried out on the enemys trench system with good effect Destructive shoots were also carried on in conjunction with the Infantry and 'K' Special Coy R.E. Observation in this Sector was good and consequently the shooting at all times was accurate & most effective.	R.T.D.

Confidential

War Diary

of the

127th Light Trench Mortar Battery

from

July 1st 1918

to

July 31st 1918

Volume 2.

WAR DIARY
or
INTELLIGENCE SUMMARY.

Army Form C. 2118.

Place	Date	Hour	Summary of Events and Information	Remarks and references to Appendices
In the line (Battery Hq J.24.d)	1-7-18		Reference Sheet 57D 1:40,000. In conjunction with a raid on LA SIGNY FARM, 300 rounds were fired on prearranged target.	D.H.1
do	2-7-18 to 10-7-18		Dispositions of the mortars was changed during this period, all except two being withdrawn to defended localities for purposes of defence. A great deal of work was accomplished towards the completion of Gun pits, Ammunition recesses and shelters in these localities. A considerable amount of offensive firing on enemy Infantry posts was also carried out. Good observation was obtained and on several occasions the enemy was obviously hit in tender spots. An average of 100 rounds per day was fired.	D.H.1
Bus Woods (J.20.c)	10-7-18		Battery was relieved by the 125th L.T.M.B. Relief complete by 4 p.m. Battery proceeded to BUS WOODS (J.20.c)	D.H.1
do	10-7-18 to 18-7-18		The Brigade was in Divisional Reserve and the defensive role of the Battery was studied & practised. Sites were chosen for Gun positions in the Reserve line and Ammunition was carried by limber to these places and stored in prepared recesses. Setting-up drill was carried out. Divisional Baths were made use of and all necessary re-acquipment was completed.	D.H.1

WAR DIARY
or
INTELLIGENCE SUMMARY.

Army Form C. 2118.

Place	Date	Hour	Summary of Events and Information	Remarks and references to Appendices
In the line (Battery HQ at J.17.c)	18-7-18		The Battery relieved the 126th L.T.M. Battery, leaving BUS WOODS (J.20.c) at 1 p.m. Relief was complete at 4.30 p.m. Mortars were taken over as follows :- Two in S.O.S positions covering the front line, four in Defended localities in case of an enemy break-through, and two in reserve at Battery H.Q.	DA1
do	18-7-18 to 24-7-18		Consequent to the advance of our line between HEBUTERNE (K.9) and LA SIGNY FARM (K.27) four mortars were moved up into offensive positions in order to engage enemy posts which might resist. 50 Rounds were fired. Thereafter the mortars were kept in advanced positions for the defence of our outpost line	DA1
do	24-7-18 to 31-7-18		Three of the Mortars in forward positions were taken back to the defended localities to which they belonged and a fourth was put into permanent offensive position covering the Outpost line. Three new Gun pits were constructed, and many ammunition recesses were made in advanced positions to obviate the necessity of carrying forward ammunition in case of offensive fire being asked for. Ammunition was collected and made into dumps protected from exposure. A great deal of work was done on	DA1

WAR DIARY or INTELLIGENCE SUMMARY.

Army Form C. 2118.

(Erase heading not required.)

Place	Date	Hour	Summary of Events and Information	Remarks and references to Appendices
In the line (Battery HQ at J.17.c)	24-7-18 to 31-7-18		the revetting of Gun positions & trenches, drainage and improvement of shelters and Gun pits, and the collecting and renovating or salving ammunition. A strictly defensive attitude was maintained as our front systems gave little cover for offensive work and the enemy presented few targets worth engaging within range of our Mortars. Douglas K/ Cures Capt.	DK/

127th T.M. Battery. WAR DIARY August. 1918. Army Form C. 2118.
INTELLIGENCE SUMMARY.
SHEET 1.

Place	Date	Hour	Summary of Events and Information	Remarks and references to Appendices
In the line (Battery H.Q. J.7.c.)	1-8-18 to 2-8-18		MAP REF. SHEETS 57.c. 1/40.000. and 57.d. 1/40.000. Work on new gun pits & ammn. recesses continued.	AWW
do.	3-8-18		Battery relieved in the line by 125th L.T.M.B. and marched to camp in BUS WOODS. Relief complete 4.30 pm.	AWW
BUS WOODS (J.20.c.)	4-8-18 to 8-8-18		Resting & training.	AWW
do.	9-8-18		1 officer & 26 O.R. sent up the line to assist 126th T.M.B. in firing in conjunction with raid on VALLADE TRENCH c... This raid did not materialise, owing to the withdrawal of the enemy in this sector.	AWW
do.	9-8-18 to 11-8-18		Resting & training in BUS WOODS.	AWW
In the line (right sector)	12-8-18		Battery relieved 126th Light T.M.B. in the line. Relief complete 11.15 pm.	AWW
	13-8-18		In the line. Battery. H.Q. FORT BERTHA.	AWW
	14-8-18		Enemy retired from his front system. 2 guns with each of the 2 Battns. in the line.	AWW

127th T.M.B.   WAR DIARY / INTELLIGENCE SUMMARY   August, 1918 (continued).   SHEET. 2.   Army Form C. 2118.

(Instructions regarding War Diaries and Intelligence Summaries are contained in F. S. Regs., Part II. and the Staff Manual respectively. Title pages will be prepared in manuscript.)

(Erase heading not required.)

Place	Date	Hour	Summary of Events and Information	Remarks and references to Appendices
In the line (right sector).	15.8.18		Battery H.Q. moved to CHALK PIT K.32.a.4.1. Section H.Q. dugout in SERRE TRENCH. K.35.c.7.3.	AWW
do.	16.8.18		Battery H.Q. moved from CHALK PIT to dugout 200 yds. away.	AWW
do.	16.8.18 to 20.8.18		2 guns with right Battn., 2 with left Battn.. No offensive firing done beyond a few rounds.	AWW
do.	21.8.18		Attack opened by us at dawn on whole of Corps front. One gun went forward with 15 rds. of ammn. with right Battn. (1/6th Manch.). This gun did no firing. Remainder of Battery detailed to escort prisoners from the line to Divl. Cage.	AWW
do.	22.8.18 to 23.8.18		Attack continued. One gun remained with 1/6th Manch., but did no firing.	AWW
do.	24.8.18		Battery H.Q. moved to MUNICH TRENCH. Enemy again retiring.	AWW
MIRAUMONT.	25.8.18		" " " " MIRAUMONT. One gun withdrawn from 1/6th Manch..	AWW
PYS.	26.8.18		Battery marched to PYS & occupied shelters at the cemetery; M.2.d.	AWW

127th T.M.B. WAR DIARY August, 1918 (continued). SHEET 3. Army Form C. 2118.
INTELLIGENCE SUMMARY.
(Erase heading not required.)

Place	Date	Hour	Summary of Events and Information	Remarks and references to Appendices
P.Y.S.	27-8-18		Battery left P.Y.S. 10.p. and relieved 188th T.M.B. in the line in front of THILLOY. 4 guns in the line — firing from road about M.6.b.6.0. Battery H.Q. M.6. central. Section H.Q. M.6.d.5.7.	AWW
In the line (Battery H.Q. M.6 central.)	28-8-18 to 31-8-18		4 in the line. No offensive firing done.	AWW

A.W.Welch. Lieut.
for Capt.
Comdg. 127th Light T.M. Battery.

Confidential

War Diary

of the

147th Light Trench Mortar Battery

from September 1st 1918
to September 30th 1918

Volume 1.

127th Light T.M. Battery **WAR DIARY** September, 1918. Army Form C. 2118.

INTELLIGENCE SUMMARY.

(Erase heading not required.)

SHEET. 1.

Place	Date	Hour	Summary of Events and Information	Remarks and references to Appendices
			REFERENCE MAP 1/40.000 SHEET 57.c.	
In the line (Battery H.Q. M.6. central)	SEPTR. 1st.		Battery H.Q. M.6. central. Section H.Q. N.4.a.5.9. 2 guns in the line at RIENCOURT. (These guns fired 30 rds. on hostile M.G's. during night of 31st/1st.	AWW.
In the line. (H.Q. N.4.a.5.9.)	2nd.	5.15 a.m.	Battery H.Q. N.4.a.5.9. 127th Bgde. attacked & captured VILLERS - AU - FLOS. LIEUT. WELCH & 29.O.R. went over with first wave — one gun with 1/5th Bn. and one gun with 1/6th Bn.. 30 rds. ammn. with each gun, carried in each case by own carrying party of 10 men. All ammn. fired on strong points &c. during the attack. The Battery captured 25 prisoners, 2 light T.M's, 1 heavy M.G. & 2 light M.G's. Casualties, 1 killed, 8 wounded.	
		3.p.m.	Gun detachments & carrying parties withdrawn to Battery H.Q. 3.p.m.	AWW.
do.	3rd-4th.		Resting at Battery H.Q.	AWW.

127th Light T.M. Battery. WAR DIARY — September, 1918.

Sheet. 2. Army Form C. 2118.

Place	Date	Hour	Summary of Events and Information	Remarks and references to Appendices
In the line (support Bde)	Sept 5th		Resting. Battery H.Q. moved to old Batt. H.Q. at N.4a.3.8.	AHW
Little Wood (M.9.d.9.9.)	6th		Battery marched into Divl. Rest quarters at Little Wood, M.9.d.9.9.	AHW
do.	7th		Resting, bathing &c..	AHW
Warlencourt M.10.b.4.7.	8th		Battery moved to new bivouacs at Warlencourt, M.10.b.4.7.	AHW
do.	9-15th		Training. Weather rather bad, hindering training a good deal.	AHW
do.	16th		2 guns fired 76 rds. in tactical scheme with a company of 1/7th Manch. Regt.. 12 men joined Battery as Reinforcements from the Battalions.	AHW
do.	17th		Training, including special instruction of reinforcements. Weather improved.	AHW
do.	18th		do. Captain D.H. Sayers, M.C. proceeded on leave to U.K. (19.9.18 to 3.10.18). Lieut. R.H. Hacker took over command of the Battery from this date, during absence of Capt. Sayers.	
		8.p.m.	Warning order received that 42nd Divn. will relieve 37th Divn. in Havrincourt sector on 21st & 22nd inst..	AHW

127th Light T.M. Battery. WAR DIARY — September, 1918.

Sheet 3.
Army Form C. 2118.

Place	Date	Hour	Summary of Events and Information	Remarks and references to Appendices
WARLENCOURT. M.10.b.4.7.	19th		Training, including live firing.	AWW
do.	20th		— do. — — do. —	AWW
BERTINCOURT P.2.d.2.8.	21st		Division relieved 37th Divn. in left sector of CORPS front. 127th Bde. in support. Battery relieved 112th T.M. Battery in dugouts at P.2.d.2.8., proceeding by Bde. route march as far as BERTINCOURT. Relief Complete 4.pm.	AWW
do.	22nd–25th		Training etc., and reconnoitring front line & gun positions.	AWW
K.31.b.6.5	26th	10.am	LT. ZOODALL, with 18 men & 6 guns, proceeded to front line at K.34.b.9.5, and placed the 6 guns in positions there, so as to fire in conjunction with Artillery barrage on the following morning.	
		7.pm	LT. WELCH, with 5 men & 1 gun proceeded to PLACE MORTMARTRE, Q.8.d., where tanks were parked.	
		7.pm	Battery H.Q. moved to YORKSHIRE BANK, K.31.b.6.5.	AWW

127th Light T.M. Battery.   WAR DIARY   September, 1918.   Army Form C. 2118.
INTELLIGENCE SUMMARY.
Sheet. 4.

Place	Date	Hour	Summary of Events and Information	Remarks and references to Appendices
In the line (Batty. H.Q. K.31.d.6.5)	SEPTR 27th	8.24am	127th Bde. attacked & captured as far as 4th Objective in attack by IIIrd Army. 6 guns put up a barrage on HINDENBURG lines & sunken roads in K.35.a. and c. 300 rounds fired during 6 mins. barrage. 1 gun taken over in a tank, with further supply of ammn. in a second tank, the gun team following just behind the tank carrying the gun. One tank had repeated engine trouble & ultimately broke down; the other, carrying ammn. only, was hit & burnt out just before reaching 3rd Objective. The rôle of this gun was to fire from K.36.c. while the Infantry were halted at the 3rd Objective. Owing to the failure of both tanks to reach 3rd Objective no firing was possible with this gun, as the Infantry had gone forward from there by the time the gun team, with a small supply of ammn. (12 rds.) had got there. Casualties, 1.O.R. wounded at duty.	
-do.-		6 pm	One gun withdrawn to Batty. H.Q., 6 remaining at K.34.b.9.5.	AWW
-do.-	28th		In same positions, resting, cleaning guns &c.	AWW
-do.-	29th	4 pm	Battery withdrawn to P.11.a.9.4., the Division being out of the line.	AWW
P.11.a.9.4.	30th		Cleaning & washing & digging in tents.	AWW

A.W.Welsh, Lieut.,
for O.C. 127th T.M. Battery.

Confidential

War Diary

of the

19th Trench Mortar Battery

From October 1st/1918
To October 31st/1918

Volume. 2.

WAR DIARY or INTELLIGENCE SUMMARY.

Army Form C. 2118.

(Erase heading not required.)

Place	Date	Hour	Summary of Events and Information	Remarks and references to Appendices
			Map Reference, Sheet 57C, 1:40,000	A.
P.11.a.9.4	Oct 1st to 7th	-	Keen training of every description was carried on during this period.	A.
do	8th	-	The Battery as part of the Brigade marched to VILLERS PLOUICH, (R.13) leaving P.11.a at 1300 arriving at VILLERS PLOUICH at 1630, Battery H.Q. (R.8.c.8.3)	A.
VILLERS PLOUICH Map Ref Sheet 57B 1:40,000.	9th	-	The Battery as part of the Brigade marched to VAUCELLES (Ref Sheet 57B M.15.) leaving VILLERS PLOUICH (R.13.) at 0850 arriving at VAUCELLES at 1120. A Hot meal was partaken of and the Battery rested for a matter of four hours at this point. The Brigade then continued the march to ESNES (H.34) leaving VAUCELLES (M.15) at 1600 arriving ESNES (H34) at 2130, Battery Hq. N.2.b.7.6.	A.
ESNES	10th to 12th		The Battery rested & cleaned up and carried out recreational training	A.
do	13th		The Battery as part of the Brigade marched to BEAUVOIS (I.10.) leaving ESNES (H34) 1020, and arriving at BEAUVOIS (I.10) at 1300. The route on this occasion was a cross-country practically all the way. Battery H.Q. at I.10.a.6.9	A.

WAR DIARY or INTELLIGENCE SUMMARY.

Army Form C. 2118.

(Erase heading not required.)

Place	Date	Hour	Summary of Events and Information	Remarks and references to Appendices
			Map Reference Sheet 57B, 1:40,000	
BEAUVOIS (I.10.)	Oct 14 to Oct 17		Battery engaged in cleaning, smartening up and training. Whilst at BEAUVOIS (I.10) the Battery was accommodated in billets for the first time since the original attack in August.	
do	18th		Battery left BEAUVOIS (I.10.) 1530 and marched to AULICOURT FARM (I.1.a) to relieve the 126th L.T.M.B. who in turn relieved the 125 Brigade in the line, the 125 Brigade going into Divisional reserve at BEAUVOIS (I.10). Whilst at AULICOURT FARM (I.1.a) the 127 Brigade performed the rôle as Brigade in support.	
AULICOURT FARM (I.1.a)	19th		The 42nd Division, in conjunction with the Divisions on the right & left, was ordered to attack at 0200 on the morning of the 20th. The 126th Brigade was ordered to make the initial attack & take the green line while the 127 Brigade was to pass through and take the final objective four hours later. The Battery left for assembly positions at 2145 arriving there at 2330 on the morning of the 19th.	
MAROU (S.E. of SOLESMES)	20th		The attack by the 126 Brigade being successful the 127 Brigade passed through them at 0700, one gun under CAPTAIN SAYERS (17th (Reserve) SCOTTISH RIFLES) was attached to the right Battalion and one gun under LIEUTENANT GOODALL was attached to the left Battalion, both Guns going over with the first wave of the attacking Companies.	

WAR DIARY or INTELLIGENCE SUMMARY.

Army Form C. 2118.

Place	Date	Hour	Summary of Events and Information	Remarks and references to Appendices
MAROU (S.E. SOLESMES)	Oct 20/21st		Both Guns were used to the utmost advantage and succeeded in firing off all their ammunition with good results. The carrying parties were both found by the Battery. Having expended all available ammunition the O.C. Battery withdrew the Guns and established Battery H.Q. at E.14.a.4.0 at 1100. The Guns were finally withdrawn by 1400 hours. Casualties – 2 ORs killed, 1 Officer 3 ORs wounded. The disposition of the Battery remained the same during the night 20th/21st and the morning of the 21st. LIEUTENANT WELCH from rear H.Q. reported to advanced Battery H.Q. on the evening of the 20th. During the Battle LIEUTENANT HACKER (1/7th MANCHESTERS) performed the duties of Liaison Officer with the 185 Infantry Brigade on the left. The Battery was relieved at 1800 by the 125 L.T.M.B. and the Battery moved back to AULICOURT FARM (I.1.a) staying there for the night 21st/22nd.	A
AULICOURT FARM (I.1.a)	22nd		The Battery as part of the Brigade marched down to Billets at BEAUVOIS (I.10) leaving AULICOURT FARM at 1515 arriving BEAUVOIS (I.10) 1615. Battery H.Q. I.10.a.4.7	A
BEAUVOIS (I.10)	23rd/31st		Battery engaged resting, cleaning up and keen training of every description and re-organization.	

R Heathcote Hackney
Lt.

WAR DIARY or INTELLIGENCE SUMMARY.

Army Form C. 2118.

127th Tm Bty

Place	Date	Hour	Summary of Events and Information	Remarks and references to Appendices
BEAUVOIS (5.E.)	Nov 1st to Nov 3rd	—	Reference Sheet VALENCIENNES 1:100,000. Battery engaged in training and organizing for the move forward.	R.A.
	- 3		Battery as part of the Brigade, marched to VIESLEY (5.f.) leaving BEAUVOIS (5.e.) at 2100 and arriving VIESLEY (5.f.) at 2300 hours	R.A.
VIESLEY (5.f.)	- 4		The march forward was continued; the Battery leaving VIESLEY (5f) at 1300 marched to VERTIGNEUL FARM (4.g.) arriving there at 1600.	R.A.
VERTIGNEUL FARM (4.g.)	- 5		Battery left VERTIGNEUL FARM (4.g.) at 0935 marched to FME-DU-LION (4.i.) arriving there at 1635.	R.A.
FME du LION (4.i.)	- 6		Battery left FME du LION (4.i.) at 0830 and marched to cross roads in the FORET de MORMAL (4.i.9.8) arriving there at 1130. At this time the 126th Brigade had passed through the N.Z. DIVISION the 127th Brigade being in support. At 1500 same day the Battery was ordered to return to MAISON ROUGE (4.i.) arriving there at 1540 and becoming Brigade in reserve.	R.A.
MAISON ROUGE (4.i.)	- 7		Battery spent the day in cleaning and drying. The weather up to this time had been very wet and conditions generally were bad.	R.A.

WAR DIARY / INTELLIGENCE SUMMARY

Army Form C. 2118.

Place	Date	Hour	Summary of Events and Information	Remarks and references to Appendices
MAISON ROUGE (4.i)	Nov 8th		Battery marched from MAISON ROUGE at 0830 and arrived at VIEUX-MESNIL (3.k) at 1515.	R.H.
VIEUX MESNIL (3.k)	9th to 12th		Battery resting, cleaning up and recreational training	R.H.
do	13th		The Battery as part of the Brigade marched to Billets in HAUTMONT (3.l) leaving VIEUX-MESNIL at 1000 and arriving at HAUTMONT 1145 hours.	R.H.
HAUTMONT (3.l)	14th to 30th		Battery engaged in keen training, route marching and smartening up generally. Preparations for Education, demobilization and a further move forward were made.	R.H.

R. Heathcote Harkins

Confidential

War Diary

of the

127th Light Trench Mortar Battery

from

November 1st/918

to

November 30th/918

Volume. 2.

<u>Confidential</u>

War Diary
for
127th L.T.M Battery
1st - 31st December 1918.

Volume 12.

WAR DIARY / INTELLIGENCE SUMMARY

Army Form C. 2118.

Place	Date	Hour	Summary of Events and Information	Remarks and references to Appendices
HAUTMONT (Ref. Sheet Valenciennes 1:100,000) 3B.	Dec 1 to Dec 13		Reference Sheet NAMUR 8. 1/100,000 Battery engaged in keen training, smartening up and education. Preparations for the move forward were made.	R.A.
HAUTMONT	14		The Battery as part of the Brigade marched to BOUSSOIS (3A) arriving there at 1330 hrs. Having left HAUTMONT at 0900 hrs.	R.A.
BOUSSOIS (3A)	15		Battery left BOUSSOIS at 0900 hrs. and marched to MERBES-ST.-MAIRE (2c) arriving there at 1400 hrs.	R.A.
MERBES ST MAIRE (2c)	16		Battery left MERBES-ST-MAIRE (2c) at 1100 hrs. and marched to LEVAL-TRAHEGNIES (1c) arriving there at 1430 hrs.	R.A.
LEVAL TRAHEGNIES (1c)	17		The Battery spent the day resting and cleaning up.	R.A.
LEVAL TRAHEGNIES	18		Battery left LEVAL-TRAHEGNIES (1c) at 0900 hrs. and marched to MARCHIENNES-AU-PONT (2E) arriving there at 1330 hrs.	R.A.
MARCHIENNES AU PONT	19		Battery left MARCHIENNES-AU-PONT at 0930 hrs and marched to FLEURUS (1G) arriving there at 1330 hrs.	R.A.

WAR DIARY ~~INTELLIGENCE SUMMARY~~

Army Form C. 2118.

(Erase heading not required.)

Place	Date	Hour	Summary of Events and Information	Remarks and references to Appendices
FLEURUS (IG)	Dec 20th to 31st		<u>Reference Sheet NAMUR 8 1·100,000</u> During the march the conditions were good. Battery was engaged in individual training, smartening up, and education. Demobilization was commenced. R. Heathcote Hacker.	

www.ingramcontent.com/pod-product-compliance
Lightning Source LLC
Chambersburg PA
CBHW081238170426
43191CB00034B/1975